HOW TO SET UP A

REAL ESTATE INVESTMENT TRUST

What You Need To Know

P. C. Pride

E-MAIL: PCOPRIDE@GMAIL.COM

COPYRIGHT © 2016   ALL RIGHTS RESERVED.

No part of this publication may be reproduced, stored in a retrieval system, or transmitted in any form or by any means, electronic, mechanical, photocopying, recording or otherwise without the prior written permission of the author.

ISBN:

ISBN-13:978-1517605667

ISBN-10:1517605660

Warning and Disclaimer

Every effort has been made to make this book as complete and as accurate as possible, but no warranty is implied. The information provided is on an "as is' basis. The author and the publisher shall have neither liability nor responsibility to any person or entity with respect to any loss or damages arising from the information contained in this book.

Table of Contents

1. What is an REIT — 3
2. REIT Regulatory Requirements — 5
3. Steps to Setting Up An REIT — 6
4. Evaluating Real Estate Investment Clubs — 8
5. Types of Commercial Property — 10
6. Types of Commercial Leases — 22
7. Finding Properties — 24
8. Commercial Real Estate Auctions — 26
9. Types of REITs — 28
10. Publicly Traded & Non-Publicly Traded REITS- — 30
11. Financing An REIT — 33
12. Selecting Commercial Properties: — 37
13. Risk Analyses -Operational — 38
14. Return On Investment — 41
15. Appendix: Additional Resources

Chapter 1: What is an REIT?

The Security and Exchange Commission defines Real Estate Investment Trusts (REITs) as a company that owns and typically operates income-producing real estate or real estate-related assets.

REITs allow individuals to share income from their investment in large scale income-producing property without actually having to go out and buy the property.

REITs originated over 100 years ago. In the 1880s REITs could then avoid double taxation, i.e. corporate tax and individual tax. However, in the 1930's this tax advantage was removed.

In 1960 President Dwight Eisenhower signed into law an REIT tax provision which was contained in a Cigar Excise Tax. Owners now would not face the double tax as long as the bulk of the income from an income producing property is distributed to the investors.

Now, more than fifty years later there are over 300 REITs listed on the New York Stock Exchange. According to the National Association of REITs (NAREIT), the industry has 1.7 trillion in gross assets and employs one million people.

REITs enable small investors to commit as little as $500, $2500, $50,000 or more in an REIT and over time receive monthly, quarterly and annual dividends to supplement their income. While risk is fairly low and the REIT does not pay corporate tax. The investor does pay income tax on the income gained from an REIT payout.

REITs invest in shopping malls, self storage, apartments, warehouses, warehousing facilities, hospitals and clinics, senior living facilities, offices, data centers, telecommunication towers, retail, hotels, timber producing land and office buildings to name a few.

There are over 40,000 REIT owned properties in the US and there are over thirty foreign countries who have adopted the United States REIT model.

NAREIT notes that returns on investment for the past 20 years at 16% for self storage, Residential 12%, Retail 12%, Healthcare 13% and office buildings 12%. Public REITs paid out $ 34 billion in 2013.

Chapter 2: REIT Regulatory Requirements

To qualify as a REIT, a company must have the bulk of its assets and income connected to real estate investment and must distribute at least 90 percent of its taxable income to shareholders annually in the form of dividends.

In addition to paying out at least 90 percent of its taxable income annually in the form of shareholder dividends, a REIT must:

- Be an entity that would be taxable as a corporation but for its REIT status
- Be managed by a board of directors or trustees
- Have shares that are fully transferable
- Have a minimum of 100 shareholders after its first year as a REIT
- Have no more than 50 percent of its shares held by five or fewer individuals during the last half of the taxable year
- Invest at least 75 percent of its total assets in real estate assets and cash
- Derive at least 75 percent of its gross income from real estate related sources, including rents from real property and interest on mortgages financing real property
- Derive at least 95 percent of its gross income from such real estate sources and dividends or interest from any source
- Have no more than 25 percent of its assets consist of non-qualifying securities or stock in taxable REIT subsidiaries

Source: sec.gov

Chapter 3: Steps to Set Up A REIT

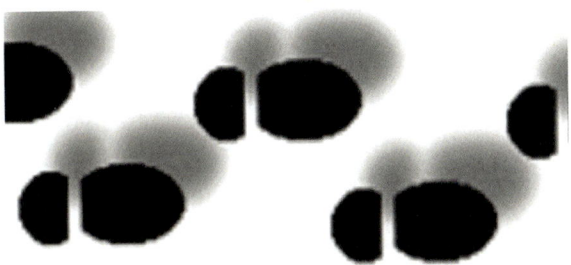

Start setting up your REIT with a Real Estate Investment Club by recruiting people in real estate, law, finance and accounting and others interested in REITs. Joining an investment club will help you to become a savvy investor.

Reasons to join a Real Estate Investment Club

- Members can obtain a portfolio of commercial real estate available for sale aligned with the group's criteria.
- Learn laws and regulations specific to real estate such as zoning & land use laws
- Learn how to crunch the numbers in real estate investing
- Risk analyses methodologies and due diligence activities
- Obtain professional, legal and financial advice
- Understand commercial markets

Sample Recruitment Letter

Letterhead

Name

Dear Sir/Ms:

What: Real Estate Investment Club

Intent: Establish a **Real Estate Investment Trust** regulated by the Securities and Exchange Commission

Process: To meet and learn more about Real Estate Investments and REITs with guest speakers from the legal, accounting, investing and real estate community. Learn to evaluate and select properties for purchase.

When: Day, Date, Time

Location:

Directions:

Questions: Tel: Cell: Email:

(List you classes and potential monthly calendar of activities)

Chapter 4: Evaluating Real Estate Investment Clubs

If you are new to investing then joining an investment club is an excellent way to learn about investing in REITs. Evaluate several clubs before settling on one or two. Use the following criteria.

- ✓ Number of people in the club

- ✓ Review their written bylaws

- ✓ Make sure they are incorporated or are in the process of doing so.

- ✓ Determine if the clubs purpose/mission is in line with the return on investment you are seeking.

- ✓ Determine meeting schedule and what workshops are being provided.

- ✓ Review level of participation.

- ✓ Assess the knowledge transferred in each group meeting.

- ✓ Become a more savvy investor in social sessions discussing investing in REITs

- ✓ Rotate speakers from the group so all persons participate

- ✓ Find new real estate investment opportunities

- ✓ Participate in online and offline discussions

- ✓ Establish an investment strategy and work to obtain results.

Avoid scams for clubs that ask for more than $50 to $200 dollars annually.

A good way to find and analyze investment clubs is to visit Real Estate forums and websites. Here you can read reviews, watch videos and search for guest speakers who can answer your questions. Take a look at the following websites to expand your knowledge.

State by State Guide to Real Estate Investment Clubs

http://www.reiclub.com/real-estate-clubs.php - Website has a list of 230 plus Real Estate Investment Clubs.

http://www.reiclub.com/real-estate-clubs.php
List clubs by state as well as a plethora of informative investor information.

http://www.nationalreia.com/
Provides a list of clubs and a guide to starting an investment club

http://www.money-zine.com/investing/investing/real-estate-investment-clubs/
Provides information to the 150 Real Estate Investment Clubs

http://home.howstuffworks.com/real-estate/buying-home/real-estate-investment-clubs1.htm
Provides information on starting your own Investment Club

Chapter 5: Types of Commercial Property

Commercial real estate can be broken down into several different categories. When people think of different types of commercial real estate, they typically think about shopping centers, office buildings, or warehouses. But the commercial real estate industry is much more precise when it comes to defining property types. Below is a list of different types of commercial real estate with a description of how each category is typically defined.

OFFICE

Classification - Office buildings are grouped into one of three categories: Class A, Class B, or Class C. Class A buildings are considered the best of the best in terms of construction and location. Class B properties have high quality construction, but the location is less desirable. Class C offices do not fall into either category.

Central Business District (CBD) - Office buildings located in the central business district are in the heart of a city. In larger cities like Chicago or New York, and in some medium sized cities like Boston, or Miami, these buildings would include highrises found in downtown areas.

Suburban Office Buildings - This classification of office space generally includes midrise structures of 80,000-400,000 square feet located outside of a city center. Cities will also often have suburban office parks which assemble several different midrise buildings into a campus-like setting.

Office buildings reflect the ups and downs of the market and the growth of the demand for office workers. Maintenance of offices buildings are high and can have a substantial impact on return on investments (ROI).

INDUSTRIAL

Heavy Manufacturing -This category of industrial property is really a special use category that most manufacturers would fall under. These types of properties are heavily customized with machinery for the end user, and usually require substantial renovation to re-purpose for another tenant.

Light Assembly - These structures are much simpler than the above heavy manufacturing properties, and usually can be easily reconfigured. Typical uses include storage, product assembly, and office space.

Flex warehouse - Flex space is industrial property that can easily be converted and normally includes a mix of both industrial and office space.

Bulk Warehouse - These properties are very large, normally in the range of 50,000-1,000,000 square feet. Often these properties are used for regional distribution of products and require loading docks and easy access for trucks entering and exiting highway systems.

RETAIL

Strip Center - Strip centers are smaller retail properties that may or may not house an anchor (a large retail tenant) which usually serves to draw customers into the property. Examples of anchor tenants are Wal-Mart, Publix, or Home Depot. Strip centers typical contain a mix of small retail stores like restaurants, dry cleaners, nail salons or clothing boutiques.

Community Retail Center- Community retail centers are normally in the range of 150,000-350,000 square feet. Multiple anchors occupy community centers, such as grocery stores and drug stores. Additionally, it is common to find one or more restaurants located in a community retail center.

Power Center - A power center generally has several smaller, inline retail stores, but is distinguished by the presence of a few major box retailers, such as Wal-Mart, Lowes, Staples or Best Buy. Each big box retailer usually occupies between 30,000-200,000 square feet, and these retail centers typically contain several out parcels.

Regional Mall - Malls range from 400,000-2,000,000 square feet and generally have a handful of anchor tenants such as department stores or big box retailers like Barnes & Noble or JC Penney.

Out parcel - Most large retail centers contain one or more out parcels, which are parcels of land which is set aside for individual tenants such as fast-food restaurants or banks.

    You will note that if you have the right location, visibility, population density, population growth and relative income levels plus an anchor, the Retail properties have a better return on investment and offer more stable income flow than office buildings. The leases are generally longer and there is little turnover.

Multifamily

Garden Apartments -Starting in the 1960's & 1970s suburban garden apartments began to populate the housing landscape. Apartments often contain 50-400 units and usually are 3-4 stories. Generally there is little surface parking and no elevators.

Midrise Apartments - These properties are usually 5-9 stories, with between 30-110 units, and have elevator service. These are often constructed in urban infill locations.

Highrise Apartments - Highrise apartments are found in larger markets. They usually have 100 or more units, and are professionally managed.

Multifamily- Residential properties are the most stable investment in a portfolio. People will always need a place to live and operating expenses can be passed onto the tenant.

Hotels

Full service hotels- Full service hotels are located in central business districts or tourist areas and include big name hospitality icons such as the Four Seasons, Marriott, or Ritz Carlton.

Limited service hotels - Hotels in the limited service category are usually boutique properties. These limited service hotels are often smaller and provide fewer amenities such as room service, on-site restaurants, or convention space.

Extended stay hotels - These hotels have larger rooms, small kitchens, and are designed for people staying a week or more.

Land

Greenfield Land -Greenfield refers to pastures or farm land that is undeveloped.

Infill Land - Infill land is located in a city which was previously developed, but is now vacant.

Brownfield Land - Brownfields are parcels of land previously used for industrial or commercial purposes, but are now available for re-use. These properties are generally environmentally impaired.

Special Purpose - Examples of special purpose commercial real estate include self-storage, car washes, theme parks, bowling alleys, marinas, theaters, funeral homes, community centers, nursing homes, and churches.

Mixed-Use Properties- Properties which are residential and commercial space with retail and office buildings.

The above categories of real estate cover the major types of commercial real estate. However, there are plenty of other types of commercial real estate that investors construct and own such as pipelines and cell phone towers.

Chapter 6: Types of Commercial Leases

Commercial leases typically break down into 3 major categories, with a few variations depending on property type and individual properties. They each revolve around the base rental rate and how the properties operating expenses are passed down to each tenant in the building.

Full Service – typically means the asking rental rate of the property includes all operating expenses the property owes such as janitorial services, property maintenance, utilities, and property taxes. This is the simplest and most undisguised form of a commercial lease and is most common in multi-tenant office properties catering to smaller tenancy (1-15 person businesses).

While a full service lease has the vast majority of additional operating expenses already baked into the monthly rent, the language within the lease typically states that the landlord has the right to pass down to the tenants any future increases in those expenses on a pro rata basis. So, for example during the summer months when a building will typically push out more air conditioning, the property's A/C expense will likely be over what they estimate (based on the previous year's bills) and the tenants will receive a bill.

Triple Net Lease – commonly listed as "NNN" on available space listings, refers to properties whose asking rental rate is not inclusive of the additional operating expenses tenants can expect to incur renting space. Net leases are very common in retail properties or free standing properties, but are also beginning to become prevalent in traditional multi-tenant office properties as well. NNN expenses may include expenses such as real estate taxes, insurance, maintenance, repairs, utilities, and other items.

The "net" operating expenses categories are utilities, maintenance, property taxes, insurance and sometimes management. Owners typically bill their tenants each month for these extra expenses in addition to the rent.

These additional operating expenses can vary from property to property, but prospective tenants can typically add $10-$15 per square foot in annual rental rates to get an idea of total cost picture.

Modified Gross - sometimes referred to as "Industrial Gross", this type of lease is most common with industrial or warehouse space. In most cases, tenants of industrial properties will have a full service lease that's been modified so that some of the expense categories (usually electrical) will be charged in addition to monthly rent. All other property expenses are already included in the regular monthly rent.

Percentage Lease – the tenant is responsible for paying base rent on the property, as well as a monthly % of revenue earned from the business occupying the rented space. They are most often used in retail spaces and specifically malls.

Chapter 7: Finding Properties

Identifying and having commercial real estate professionals as a part of your REIT team is essential. A series of meeting should cover the various types of properties and where to find them. Searching the numerous commercial real estate databases will give your organization an excellent way to get started identifying properties to be considered for investment.

You will be able to search by property type, location, zipcode, square footage. The best strategy is to know a number of commercial real estate brokers who are familiar with your investment area and can also help you with evaluating and determining appropriate value for an offer to purchase.

Commercial Real Estate Search Engines

http://www.loopnet.com

http://showcase.com

http://www.cimls.com/

http://www.cityfeet.com/

http://home.remaxcommercial.com

http://commercialsearch.realtor.com/

http://www.cbcworldwide.com/

http://www.thalhimer.com/

http://www.catylist.com/

http://www.cbre.us/Pages/Home.aspx

https://www.reis.com/

http://www.croesusplace.com/

http://www.nytimes.com/pages/realestate/commercial/index.html

http://www.colliers.com/en-us

http://kwcommercial.com/commercial/index.html

http://officespace.oodle.com/for-lease/retail-property-for-rent/

https://www.costar.com/

http://www.commercialsearch.com/

National Real Estate Investor: nreionline.com

http://www.buildingsearch.com/

http://nreionline.com/

8. Commercial Real Estate Auctions

Just as you can find bargains at residential real estate auctions, you can find commercial real estate bargains.

http://auctions.com
http://www.hubzu.com
https://bankassetpoint.com
http://www.propertyauction.com/
http://www.loopnet.com/Commercial-Auctions/
http://www.williamsauction.com/commercial-real-estate-auction
http://www.tranzon.com/OnLineAuctions.aspx
http://www.keyauctioneers.com/auction-search/commercial-real-estate-auctions/
https://www.treasury.gov/auctions/treasury/rp/realprop.shtml
http://www.auctionzip.com/realestate.htm
https://www.auctionnetwork.com/

Auction Terminology
http://www.realtor.org/auction/glossary
http://www.sothebys.com/en/Glossary.html
http://www.auctionadvisory.com/glossary.htm
http://www.auction.com/lp/legal/auction-terms/

Auction Advantages
http://www.frontdoor.com/real-estate/advantages-and-disadvantages-of-buying-a-foreclosure

Buying Foreclosures
http://www.ccim.com/cire-magazine/articles/auction-advantage
http://www.realtytrac.com/real-estate-guides/how-to-buy-foreclosures/bank-owned-homes/bank-owned-reo-property-faqs/
http://foreclosures.bankofamerica.com/
http://reo.wellsfargo.com/
https://www.homepath.com/
http://www.us.hsbc.com/
http://www.bbt.com/bbtdotcom/applications/specialassets/search.page
http://www.thebankforeclosureguide.com/citibank-foreclosure-listings/

http://www.realtytrac.com/mapsearch/bank-owned-properties
http://www.bankreorealestate.com/bank-reo-list
http://www.realtor.org/auction/the-basics-benefits
http://www.realtor.org/auction/types-of-auctions

http://www.realtor.org/auction/grab-the-auction-opportunity
http://www.frontdoor.com/real-estate/advantages-and-disadvantages-of-buying-a-foreclosure

Chapter 9: Types of REITs

Many REITs are registered with the SEC and are publicly traded on a stock exchange. These are known as publicly traded REITs. Others may be registered with the SEC but are not publicly traded. These are known as non- traded REITs (also known as non-exchange traded REITs). This is one of the most important distinctions among the various kinds of REITs. Before investing in a REIT, you should understand whether or not it is publicly traded, and how this could affect the benefits and risks to you.

Three Categories of REITs

REITs generally fall into three categories: equity, mortgage, and hybrid REITs. Most REITs are equity REITs.

Equity REITs typically own and operate income-producing real estate. Mortgage REITs on the other hand, provide money to real estate owners and operators either directly in the form of mortgages or other types of real estate loans, or indirectly through the acquisition of mortgage-backed securities.

Mortgage REITs tend to be more leveraged (that is, they use a lot of borrowed capital) than equity REITs. In addition, many mortgage REITs manage their interest rate and credit risks through the use of derivatives and other hedging techniques. You should understand the risks of these strategies before deciding to invest in these types of REITs.

Hybrid REITs generally are companies that use the investment strategies of both equity REITs and mortgage REITs.

Because they often invest in debt securities secured by residential and commercial mortgages, Hybrid REITs can be similar to certain investment companies that are focused only on real estate.

Generally, companies that invest a majority of their assets in real estate are exempted from the rules that govern investment companies, such as mutual funds.

The Securities and Exchange Commission has initiated a review to determine whether certain mortgage REITs should continue to be exempt from investment company regulation. Those rules generally limit the amount of leverage that a fund can use and regulate the fees that can be charged to investors.

Chapter 10: Publicly Traded REITs and Non-Traded REITs

The table below compares the characteristics of publicly traded and non-traded REITs.

Publicly Traded REITs

Overview
REITs that file reports with the SEC and whose shares trade on national stock exchanges.

Liquidity
Shares are listed and traded, like any publicly traded stock, on major stock exchanges. Most are listed on the New York Stock Exchange NYSE

Transaction Costs
Brokerage costs the same as for buying or selling publicly traded stock

Management
Typically, the managers are employees of the company.

Minimum Investment Amount
One share

Independent Directors
Stock exchange rules require a majority of directors to be independent of management. NYSE and NASDAQ rules call for a fully independent audit, nominating, and compensation committees

Investor Control
Investors elect directors

Corporate Governance
Specific stock exchange rules on corporate governance.

Disclosure Obligation
Required to make regular SEC disclosures including quarterly financial reports and yearly audited financial reports

Share Value Transparency
Real-time market prices are publicly available
Wide range of analyst reports available to the public

Non-Traded REITS

REITs that file reports with the SEC but whose shares do not trade on national stock exchanges.

Shares are not traded on public stock exchanges. Redemption programs for shares vary by company and are typically very limited. Investors may have to wait to receive a return of their capital until the company decides to engage in a transaction such as the listing of the shares on an exchange or a liquidation of the company's assets.

Typically, fees of 9 - 10 percent of the investment are charged for broker-dealer commissions and other upfront offering costs. Ongoing acquisition and management fees and other expenses are also typical. Back-end fees may be charged.

Typically, the company has no employees and is managed by a third party pursuant to a management contract.

Investment: Typically, $1,000 - $2,500.

North American Securities Administrators Association ("NASAA") guidelines, which have been adopted by many states, require a majority of directors to be independent of management. NASAA guidelines also require that a majority of each board committee consist of independent directors

Investors elect directors
Corporate governance is subject to state and NASAA guidelines. Required to make regular SEC disclosures, including quarterly financial reports and yearly audited financial reports

Share value transparency- offers no independent information about share value. Company may provide an estimated share value 18 months after the offering has closed.

Source: National Association of Real Estate Investment Trusts (NAREIT)

Chapter 11: Financing A REIT

It would be best if the members pooled their funds and paid cash for a property. Most ask for an investment of $5000.00 or more.

Crowdfunding

New to Real Estate Financing is Crowdfunding a game changing platform for investors. Crowdfunding is a method of raising capital through contributions from friends, family, customers, and individual investors. In 2013, the crowdfunding industry raised over $5.1 billion worldwide.

Through crowdfunding, investors pool money together and buy shares of real property without having to manage the property themselves or deal with any of the day-to-day management of the property. Investors use a single purpose LLC to pool money to buy real estate. Payout is generally in 18-24 months.

Here are a few Real Estate crowd-funding website. Combining the best of crowd sourcing and micro finance, crowd-funding brings together various individuals who commit money to projects and companies they want to support. Crowd-funding is making a major impact on how people invest their money.

Real Estate Crowd-funding Resources

1. Realty Mogul - https://www.realtymogul.com/

2. Fundrise - https://fundrise.com/

3. Groundbreaker - https://www.groundbreaker.co/

4. CrowdStreet - https://www.groundbreaker.co/

5. Groundfloor - https://www.groundfloor.us/

6. iFunding - https://www.ifunding.co/

8. RealCrowd - https://www.realcrowd.com/

9. Realty Shares - https://www.realtyshares.com/

10. Patch of Land - https://patchofland.com/

11. Prodigy Network https://www.prodigynetwork.com/default.aspx

12. American Homeowner Preservation- https://ahpinvest.com/

13. Lending Club - https://www.lendingclub.com/

14. Angel Capital Association
http://www.angelcapitalassociation.org/directory/

15. Realcrowd.com
https://www.realcrowd.com/offerings/register

Chapter 12: Selecting Commercial Properties: Due Diligence

When selecting properties it is imperative that physical as well as an extensive indepth analyses of the property is assessed. Also to be considered are legal issues and valuation.

Prior to any purchase, hire an inspector to generate reports on the condition of the building. Carefully review these reports and get any clarifications in writing. This is vital information which will help you to determine any immediate or future repairs, renovations and upgrades to the interior and exterior of the building. Below is a physical list to determine the viability of a commercial building.

Systems Analysis:

Roof: Age of roof and remaining life left in a roof as well as condition to determine if imminent repairs need to be made. Fortunately, today drones can provide photos.

Heat & Air – Check to see if you have the most efficient commercial HVAC system, particularly split systems. What fuels the system gas, oil, coal, electricity or other?

Electric: According to the US Energy Information Administration in 2014 Residential and Commercial electric consumption totaled 41% of all usage.

You most certainly want a licensed electrician to inspect your wiring for common electrical problems, particularly looking for knob and tube wiring. This wiring used before 1950 does not carry all the appliances we have today and can often cause fires.

Moreover, when renovating, the building may not past code and most hazard insurance companies may deny coverage.

Plumbing: Major plumbing repairs mostly come from water damage due to a pipe burst, city sewer collapse, corroded pipes and tree roots.

Interior: Check for any signs of wear and tear to floors, walls, doors and windows

Radon, Asbestos, Mold, Lead: Check current local, state and Environmental Protection Agency regulations regarding these and possibly other toxins.

Exterior: Check for structural issues, landscaping, views, easy access and most certainly parking.

Legal & Financial Due Diligence

Legal: Legal issues associated with commercial property include zoning, land use and building codes. Other legal factors to consider include property taxes, ownership, insurance(s), and boundary disputes. Working with a commercial real estate attorney enables you to obtain all background research on the property including surveys, title insurance, any liens that exist which may transfer with the title such as a mechanical lien.

Valuation: What is the appraised value of the type of commercial building? Use an experienced commercial real estate appraiser to determine the value of the building.

Contracts: Check all service contracts and any contracts disputes.

Leases: Review all leases. This is certainly necessary if you are leasing. Best to hire a Certified Public Accountant (CPA) to audit financial records including tax filings.

Parking: Retail and residential parking and its availability can help investors get higher rent. Determining the availability of onsite parking and the parking spaces which come with the building is essential.

Chapter 13: Risk Analyses-Operational

The first step to limit risk is to ensure your REIT qualifies for corporate tax exemption and meets SEC qualifying guidelines. In addition, review the following government resources that enable REITs to meet regulatory requirements.

Investor.gov website includes a broker check searchable database with background reports on investment advisers, public disclosure information, and determination if representatives are properly registered on the ADV form - www.adviserinfo.sec.gov.

The ADV form provides advisor business information and any regulatory issues. The form also provides a copy of advisor brochures describing their business practices, fees, conflicts of interest and disciplinary information.

Investor.gov also provides a list of some 19 professional designations and their meanings for investment professionals. A link to State Securities regulators of securities, broker/dealers, broker dealer agents, investment advisers and their representatives is listed.

Moreover, investor.gov is where you can learn about investing and see enforcement actions. You can see if the firm you are considering is a member of Securities Investor Protection Corporation (SIPC). This agency provides limited customer protection if a brokerage firm becomes insolvent.

The federal government's sec.gov provides Investor Education and Advocacy *Investor Alerts*, discloses recent investment frauds and scams, and issues Investor Bulletins which focuses on topical issues including recent Commission actions.

EDGAR (Electronic Data Gathering, Analysis and Retrieval) http://sec.gov/edgar/searchedgar/webusers.htm This SEC database provides free public access to corporate information. The system allows you to research a company's activities, registration statements, prospectuses, and periodic reports, which includes financial statements.

Also crowdfunding investors can use the resources of FINRA. http://www.finra.org/investors/alerts/crowdfunding-and-jobs-act-what-investors-should-know

Other risk factors in investing in REITs according to the SEC are related to market demands and include the following.

- ✓ Demand for rental space
- ✓ General real estate market factors, including an increase in market
- ✓ interest rates
- ✓ Ability to maintain rental rates
- ✓ Financial health of major tenants
- ✓ Availability and creditworthiness of prospective tenants
- ✓ Impact of consumer use of Internet E-commerce
- ✓ Impact of tenant bankruptcy
- ✓ Access to financing
- ✓ Ability to meet debt service requirements

Non-traded REITs Risk

According to the Securities and Exchange Commission non-traded REITs have some cons you should consider. Non-traded REITs are illiquid. You will most likely not be able to sell an asset quickly.

Distributions paid from loans and offering proceeds rather than income from the property, drive down the value of shares and cash is not available to the company to purchase other properties.

More importantly because they are not traded on the public exchange the value of the investment is difficult to determine. There is also the question of upfront fees which range from 9% to 15% and external manager's fees, all of which significantly reduce return on investments.

According to the SEC certain securities offerings that are exempt from registration may only be offered to, or purchased by, persons who are **accredited investors**. One principal purpose of the accredited investor concept is to identify persons who can bear the economic risk of investing in these unregistered securities.

An *accredited investor*, in the context of a natural person, includes anyone who:
- ✓ **earned income that exceeds $200,000 (or $300,000 together with a spouse) in each of the prior two years, and reasonably expects the same for the current year, OR**
- ✓ **a net worth over $1 million, either alone or together with a spouse (excluding the value of the person's primary residence).**

To learn more about non-traded REIT risks view a tip sheet from FINRA.org. http://www.finra.org/investors/alerts.

Chapter 14: Return on Investment for REIT

Building a Real Estate Investment club begins with the process for setting up an REIT. Set up your website and meet with potential investors on and offline. A learning curve will help your Investment Club and REIT have the best chance for success.

Workshops Online/Offline provide information on buying, selling, renting, leasing, development and management of commercial, residential, agricultural and other kinds of property as it relates to building a portfolio.

When membership has reached 100 or more investors can begin selecting properties, talking with commercial brokers and meeting SEC qualifications, writing bylaws, incorporating, appointing a Board of directors, writing a mission statement/business plan, filing with a State Corporation, finding a management team, filing quarterly, annual reports, filing IRS form 1120 to get REIT status which identifies the entity as an REIT and exempt from corporate taxes.

What type of payout can an investor expect? Let's say an REIT has a closing price of 30.10 on the New York Stock Exchange. Shares are traded in blocks of 100 which is the purchase of 100 units (shares) is $ 3,100.00 giving a yield of 5% or $310.00 per year. Keep investing until you have $10,000 shares with now becomes a tidy income of $31,000.

While there are no guarantees, REITs traded on the stock exchange rarely drop to 0 as REITs are based in Real Estate, a hard asset and the real estate will still have value. Generally depending on the market the yield for REITs is 3.4% which is better than Standard & Poor's 2% yield.

REITs offer a fixed-income portfolio and are an excellent investment for those who want to invest in real estate, but do not have large sums of money, and do not want to engage in the day to day operation of dealing with collecting rents, maintenance and other management responsibilities. This allows more time for the investor to manage their portfolio.

Appendix

Additional Resources

Sample mission statements
http://www.missionstatements.com/fortune_500_mission_statements.htmlmple Mission Statements

Sample Bylaws
http://www.americantower.com/Assets/uploads/files/PDFs/investor-relations/American%20Tower%20Corporation%20Bylaws.pdf

Advantages of Commercial Property Ownership
http://www.nolo.com/legal-encyclopedia/pros-cons-investing-commercial-real-estate.html

Closing Commercial Property
http://dougcornelius.com/files/closing_commercial_real_estate_transactions.pdf

File SEC FORM 1120
http://www.irs.gov/instructions/i1120rei/ch01.html
http://www.realtor.org/research-and-statistics/research-reports/commercial-real-estate

Tools for Investors
http://www.sec.gov/investor/tools.shtml
Commercial Lending Survey
http://www.realtor.org/reports/commercial-lending-trends-survey

Broker/Dealer and Investment Advisers Information

BrokerCheck
http://www.finra.org/Investors/ToolsCalculators/BrokerCheck/ is a free tool to help investors research the professional backgrounds of current and former FINRA-registered brokerage

Investment Adviser Public Disclosure (IAPD)
http://www.adviserinfo.sec.gov/IAPD/Content/IapdMain/iapd_SiteMap.aspx

Professional Designations Database -
http://apps.finra.org/DataDirectory/1/prodesignations.aspx

State Securities Regulators,
http://www.nasaa.org/about-us/contact-us/contact-your-regulator/

Securities Investor Protection Corporation (SIPC)
http://www.sipc.com/Who/Database.aspx

144: Selling Restricted and Control Securities
sec.gov/investor/pubs/rule144.htm.

Non-traded REITs
http://www.sec.gov/oiea/investor-alerts-bulletins/ib_nontradedreits.html

REIT Glossary
https://www.reit.com/investing/reit-basics/glossary-reit-terms Glossary
Commercial Real Estate Glossaries
https://www.greenstreetadvisors.com/pdf/GSAGlossary0611.pdf
http://reitinfo.com/index.php?option=com_content&view=article&id=37

:terminology&Itemid=3

SEC Form ADV
http://www.sec.gov/answers/formadv.htm

REIT Organizations
http://www.NAREIT.com
http://www.REIT.com
http://www.reitinfo.com

Real Estate Terminology
http://www.realestateabc.com/glossary/

What Do You Think This Property Costs?
Commercial Property Valuation – cost approach, market approach, income capitalization approach

An Overview of Real Estate Contracts
Sample commercial real estate contract
http://www.nycbar.org/pdf/report/contract.pdf

An Overview of Real Estate Laws
http://real-estate-law.freeadvice.com/real-estate-law/real-estate-law/133/

Real Estate Math Calculators
Math for Appraisals, appreciation, commissions, geometry, mortgages, return on investment
http://www.ajdesigner.com/index_real_estate_investment.php

Intro to online Real Estate calculators
http://www.calculator.net/real-estate-calculator.html

Real Estate Calculator Apps

https://play.google.com/store/apps/details?id=com.snc.realestatecalculator&hl=en

Real Estate Return On Investment Calculator
https://www.calcxml.com/do/inv04

Estimating the Value of an REIT: FFO/
Determine the Funds from Operation (FFO) which is reported, but does not deduct for capital expenditures used to maintain an existing portfolio of properties giving a not so accurate picture of value.

Using Adjusted Funds from Operations (AFFO)
The AFFO of a REIT is equal to the trust's funds from operations (FFO) with adjustments made for recurring capital expenditures providing a more accurate accounting of the quality of an REIT's assets.

An Overview of the Three REITs
Look into the processes and dividends of a few major REITs.
https://en.wikipedia.org/wiki/List_of_public_REITs_in_the_United_States

Index

Additional Resources	43
Auction Advantages	27
Auction Terminology	26
Categories of REITs	28
Commercial Foreclosures	27
Commercial Real Estate Search Engines	24
Commercial Real Estate Auctions	26
Crowdfunding Resources	34
Due Diligence - Protect Yourself	35
EDGAR	39
Financing REIT	33
Gross assets	3
Guide to state REIT Clubs	8
Identifying properties	24
Legal/Financial Due Diligence	36
Non-Traded REIT	31
Non-Traded REIT Risk	40
Publicly Traded REIT	30
Regulatory Requirements	5
REIT Club evaluation	8
Club Recruitment Letter	7
REIT Defined	3
REIT Real Estate Investment Club	6
REIT setup	6
Return on Investment (ROI)	41
Risk Analyses -Operational	38
Share Value Transparency	32
Shareholders	9

Structural System Analyses	36
Taxable income	5
Types of commercial leases	22
TYpes of commercial properties	10
Types of REITs	28

Made in the USA
Lexington, KY
05 September 2017